MW01247248

鵝媽媽李歌舞集

Mother Goose Lee's
Song and Dance Anthology

王克難

Claire Wang — Lee

目　錄

夜模糊月朦朧

鵝媽媽李－春之歌

鵝媽媽不要怕

鵝媽媽不要怕
女兒兒子帶食物
新鮮蔬果一大堆
吃不完
到處送
整個屋子都受惠
女兒兒子帶食物
新鮮蔬菜果一大堆
吃不完
到處送

Afraid of Being Alone and Hungry

No worries.
Daughters and sons bring food when they visit.
Fruits, veggies, and cakes
Those I can't finish.
I donate.
Daughters and sons bring food when they visit.
Fruits, veggies, and cakes.

紫花樹屋傳人

北方小城有一老人居
它的名字叫紫花樹
裏面住著許多華僑
他們都是龍的傳人
朝夕相處不厭煩
她們愛吃中國菜
最愛吃的是什麼
燒餅油條紅燒肉
朝夕相處不厭煩
相親相愛同吃住
最愛吃的是什麼？
燒餅油條紅燒肉

The Descendents of the Dragon

In the north, there is a retirement house
It's called Jacaranda House.
Many old Chinese folks live there.
They are the descendants of the Dragon.

They stay together all the time.
They all love to eat Chinese food.
What do they like the most?
Oil Twists, Crispy Buns, and Stewed Pork.

They are together all the time.
They all love to eat Chinese food.
What do they like the most?
Wanton, Dumplings, and Crispy Onion Pancake.

水仙花

那東風吹來清涼
那小鳥啼聲悠揚
月下的花兒都入夢
只有那水仙花
自己在開放

花園裏精心培養
有機化肥好營養
又白又嫩
吐露著淡淡香

我愛那月色茫茫
我愛那夜鶯啼唱
月下的花兒都入夢
只有那水仙花
又白又嫩，吐露著淡淡香。

水仙花
我為妳歌唱

水仙花
我為妳思量
我為妳歌唱
我為妳思量。
　啊⋯⋯啊⋯⋯啊
我為妳思量
我為妳歌唱。

The Night Blossoms

The east wind is calm.
The birds singing is sweet.
All the flowers in the courtyard are sleeping
except for the Night Blossom.
It blooms gently.
It blooms steadily.
All the other flowers are sleeping
except for the Night Blossom.

It is grown with lots of effort.
Plus, excellent organic fertilizers.
White and yellow, with a delicate smell.
The Night Blossom lasts.
The Night Blossom soothes.

It is grown with lots of effort.
Plus, excellent organic fertilizers.
White and Yellow with a delicate fragrance.

The Night Blossom lasts.
The Night Blossom comforts.
The other flowers in the garden are asleep.
Only the Night Blossom is blooming.
White, yellow, and fragrant.

廉價品（夢駝鈴）

開車開到超級市場
東西那裡買得完
突然聽見唱歌聲
卡拉 OK 在播放
架上有 AI 製造
價錢非常便宜。
趕緊買下一架來
回家去安裝
兩三朋友在一起
新歌老歌一起唱
一唱幾小時下來
興緻越來越高昂
肚子餓了啥辦法？
肉湯泡麵當晚餐
清風明月當窗照
歌聲就是咱家鄉。

Quick Sale

There are so many things to buy in the big supermarket.
Suddenly, I heard a gentle cry:
A buy-one -and- get- one- free for a karaoke machine.
The new machine was small and inexpensive.
I fell under its spell and bought two.
I brought two karaoke machines home.
I set them up right away and forgot about the food.
I had ramen noodles for dinner
and sang with both machines:
One in Chinese and the other in English.
I threw the paper bowl away
and did not have to wash dishes.
What happiness that was.

小城夜風（夢駝羚）

退休老人住小城。
風吹雨打街燈黯
記得老家舊房子，
舒服沙發和墊子。

兒媳撿來老沙發
坐也坐不穩
墊子太軟掉鵝毛
令人流鼻涕。

但願回到舊家鄉
一碗泡麵也願意
新舊電視看不完
外面風雨由它去。

The Buy Nothing Sofa Bed

Today, the single-room apartment is under the weather.
It was wind and drizzle in the newly moved-in retirement city.
The street light is dim.
And I was bothered.
I remember in my old house,
there was a firm sofa and soft pillows.
Today, the buy-nothing sofa is too soft,
and the old pillows spew big down feathers.

紫花樹屋故事（小城故事）

紫花樹屋故事多
充滿了歡樂
若是妳到這裡來
驚奇特別多
走廊像畫廊，小院蜂鳥窩
老人個個興沖沖
每個都好客

紫花樹屋故事多
充滿了希望
請妳跟朋友一起來
打個電話就可。

The Story of the Jacaranda House

There are lots of stories about the Jacaranda House.
If you come and see us,
you will be happily surprised. The hallway is a gallery,
and the yard has three hummingbird nests.
The residents all have an illustrious past.
It's all worthwhile to be told.
If you listen to any of them,
you will be happily surprised.

If you come on Mondays,
you will have coffee and pancakes.
If you come on Fridays,
you will have breaded fishcakes.

老人居的婦人們 （達阪城姑娘）

老人居的婦人們
住在一起
快樂又健康
天天走路
三千步啊
風雨黃昏照常忙
你要是跟她打招呼
她必微笑回答妳。
問妳一聲好
請你回家喝杯茶呀。
順便打個小麻將。

妳如不打麻將
橋牌也可以
帶著妳的老伴
加上妳的鄰居
一起來作客
一起共度好時光。

Beautiful Old Women

They are all old and healthy.
They walk at least three thousand steps a day.
Rain and storms will not stop them
because they walk inside on treadmills
with all the gadgets to make them proud.
Suppose you see the big screen in the exercise room.
The wildflower pictures on it are contributions from our
volunteer, Maureen.
She had a 3D camera
donated by our benefactor, Aileen.

吃錯藥？（達阪城姑娘）

小屋居的一群好朋友呀
大概有時會吃錯藥。

假如跟妳做朋友呀，
必定邀妳回家喝茶
有空一起去散步呀
一條巷轉另一條。

假如她們吃錯了藥呀，
只好看妳自己運氣
見到妳呀
不理不睬。
宛如陌生人一樣。

妳只能到
隔壁辛巴克呀，
叫杯不三不四茶來喝

然後希望
她們吃對的藥
又如好人一樣。

Wrong Medication

If they become your friends, they will invite you for tea.
They will take walks with you down one lane after another.
There are stores and universities around,
as well as high schools and grade schools

If they start to quarrel, then good luck!
You'll go to Starbucks to get your cup of tea.

她不愛唱歌（黃葉舞秋風）

她不愛唱歌
但是非常愛聽
聽得好起勁
隨歌起舞
曼妙輕盈
曼妙輕盈
充滿精神。
她不愛唱歌
但是非常愛聽
聽得好起勁
隨歌起舞
曼妙輕盈
曼妙輕盈
充滿精神。

Sing, Sing

She doesn't like to sing
but likes to hear others sing.
She hears with her whole heart.
Then she dances to the music.

Look at how she dances.
Light, lithe
Look at her and listen to the singers.
Look at her dance.
Her dance is as good as the other singers' singing.

春天裏來百花香

春天裏來百花香。
白雲藍天太陽照。
大好風景太美妙。
騎著單車到處跑。
太美妙　太美妙。
人生何處不是好。
何必尋煩惱　。
何必尋煩惱。

春天裏來百花香。
白雲藍天太陽照。
大好風景太美妙。
騎著單車到處跑。
太美妙　太美妙。
人生何處不是好。
何必尋煩惱　。
何必尋煩惱。

Happy Days Are Here Again

Flowers bloom in the Spring
Birds fly and spread their wings.
The sun is high above.
Happy days are here again.

The white clouds are in the sky.
Flowers bloom, and the grass is green.
One can ride a bike to the countryside.
Happy days are here again.

Happiness is everywhere.
Happiness, as well as beauty,
Clap our hands and sing to the beat.
Happy days are here again.

不要問我要做什麼（不要問我從哪裡來）

不要問我要做什麼？
我要做我愛做的事。
我要做什麼事？
太多。太多。太多。
人的一生那麼短。
要做的事那麼多。
如果還要聽人的話去做，
那真是難過。難過。難過。

還好年紀一大
一切如煙雲　轉眼就過。
大小事件　都轉眼就過。
不再悲傷　不再煩惱
任何事件　轉眼就都過。

Don't Ask Me 1

Don't ask me where I'm from.
I am from far, far away.
I like to do things that I want.
There are too many things that I want.
Too many things.
Too many things.
Let me go and set me free.
Let me go and do my things.

Life is short, and there are so many things to do.
If one has to listen to others
to do what they want you to do.
It's simply ridiculous, ridiculous,
Ridiculous.

The good thing is when one is old,
everything passes her by quickly.
Things big or small.
They all pass one by one.
Don't fret, and don't be sad.
Everything goes by quickly.

長腿（小毛小兒郎）

她有一天突然發現
四周的人都長腿
街上走的人
個個都長腿。

老人中心的服務人員
老人中心的教練
老人中心的廚師
他們都長腿。
郎裏個郎裡個龍東強
原來她老了，身體退化了。
人老了，個子變矮了。

她有一天突然發現
四周的人都長腿
街上走的人
個個都長腿。

老人中心的服務人員

老人中心的教練
老人中心的廚師
他們都長腿。
郎裏個郎裡個龍東強

原來她老了，身體退化了。
人老了，個子變矮了。

Long Legs

She found out that everyone had long legs.
The people on the streets
Before and after, her had long legs
The volunteers in the Senior center had long legs
Her coaches had long legs
It was because she had shrunk
And her bones were collapsing,
But she is still a healthy older adult..

超級健康老人歌（恭喜恭喜恭喜妳）

家中大小一切事
全部自己來管理
煮飯、洗衣、打掃，
一星期一次大清理

門窗個個擦乾淨
垃圾天天扔出去
星期天農夫市場
總有她足跡
她是超級老人呀
超級老人。

The Song of the Super Elderly

She does everything by herself,
shops for her food,
and cleans her house,
inside and out.
She washes her dishes,
makes up her bed.
She washes her clothes.
She is a super elderly lady.

Smile and laugh if you can.
Smile and laugh all the time.
All the time.
All the time.

恭喜恭喜

每條大街小巷
每個人的嘴裡
見面第一句話
就是恭喜恭喜。
恭喜恭喜恭喜你呀
恭喜恭喜恭喜你。

冬天已到盡頭,
春天就要來臨,
溫暖的微風,
吹暖了大地。
恭喜恭喜恭喜妳呀
恭喜恭喜你。

浩浩冰雪溶解
眼看梅花吐蕊
漫漫長夜過去
聽到一聲雞啼
春光來到大地

恭喜恭喜恭喜妳呀
恭喜恭喜恭喜妳。

經過多少困難
經歷多少磨練
多少心在盼望
春天的消息
恭喜恭喜恭喜你呀
恭喜恭喜恭喜妳。

Happy Days Are Here Again 1

Gong Xi, Gong Xi, Gong Xi
On every street and in every lane
From every mouth,
the first greetings we hear
are Gong Xi, Gong Xi, Gong Xi to you!
Gong Xi, Gong Xi, Gong Xi to you and yours!

Winter is ending.
Spring is coming.
The warm spring breeze
has woken up the earth.
Gong Xi, Gong Xi, Gong Xi to you!
Gong Xi, Gong Xi, Gong Xi to you and yours!

The ice and snow have melted.
The red plum tree is blooming.
The long nights are gone.
The days are lengthening.
Gong Xi, Gong Xi, Gong Xi to you!
Gong Xi, Gong Xi, Gong Xi to you and yours!

After so many tribulations
and hardships,
our hearts are rejoicing
the promise of spring.
Gong xi, gong xi, gong xi to you!
Gong xi, gong xi, gong xi to you and yours!

恭喜發財（恭喜恭喜恭喜你）

我恭喜你發財　我恭喜你愉快
最好的請過來　不好的請走開
禮多人不怪
禮多人不怪。我祝福天下的女孩
嫁一個好男孩

兩小口子永遠在一塊兒
永遠在一塊
永遠在一塊。

我祝福你全家
財運亨通住豪宅
我祝福你家好運氣
笑口經常開
祝福你家好運氣
明天比今天更愉快！

Happy Days Are Here Again 5

Gong Xi Fa Cai (Happiness and Prosperity to You)
May you prosper
and your life be wonderful.
May the best things happen to you.
May the worst things be away from you!
Gong Xi, Gong Xi ,Gong Xi to you!
Gong Xi, Gong Xi, Gong Xi to you and yours!

May all the girls marry the best husband
and have a happy family.
May all your children be healthy and happy, be good
students at school and have good jobs
when they graduate.

May you always laugh and smile
and all the happiness in the world.
May all the good things come to you
and all the bad stuff away from you.
Gong Xi, Gong Xi, Gong Xi to you!
Gong Xi, Gong Xi, Gong Xi to you and yours!

向前走（朋友別哭）

沒有一封信
能讓他不絕望
看一看大千世界
原來像夢一場
有贏有輸
到後來春風一場

向前走
前途仍可以無量
星星仍然放光芒

Walk Forward

There is no letter to make him feel alive
There is no letter to keep him from despair.

Look at the world.
Life is but a dream
They were winning, losing.
It goes like a spring wind.

台北的天空

信好像少了　電話好像不通
這世界似乎失去了夢
她走過青春　走過年少
如今發現了藝術的寶藏

台北的天空　有年輕的笑容
有他，她們的從容
台北的天空
他們熟悉的陽光
在他們心中

如今她畫台北的天空
裏面有無窮風景的去處
一張又一張畫的永遠
永遠台北的天空。

The Skies of Taipei

The letters are sparse.
The phone calls are not answered
The world seems to have lost its dream.

She walked through youth.
She walked through adulthood.
Now, she seemed to have found.

The sky of Taipei regained its youthful smile,
and the reunion was a surprise.
The sky of Taipei has its familiar sunshine,
which brightens their heart.

Now, she paints the sky of Taipei.
It has endless scenery,
one painting after another,
forever the sky of Taipei.

安靜的夜（夜，夜，夜，夜）

她想問天他在哪裏
她想問她自己
一如她的俏皮
俏皮得幾乎傷害了自己。

想問天　想問自己
或者是迷信問宿命
放棄所有　傷害了他。
放棄所有，拋棄所有
讓自己飄流在安靜的夜裡。

放棄所有，拋棄所有
讓自己飄流在安靜的夜裡。

放棄所有，拋棄所有
讓自己飄流在安靜的夜裡。

Silent Night 1

She wanted to know where he was.
She tried to ask herself as if she was fooling herself
as if she was hurting herself.

She wants to ask the sky, to ask herself
as if everything was predestined.

She wants to give up everything that might hurt him.
She wants to tell herself:

Give up everything.
Give up everything.
Let herself drift away in the quiet night.

杯中酒　情人舊

什麼最消愁
良辰又美酒
歡怒喜樂自己感受
有多少愛情
有多少思念
一杯酒能忘憂。

什麼最消愁
創作一幅畫
大小快慢
自己作主
有多少牽掛
有多少離愁
一幅美麗的畫
能消愁。能消愁

Comforting

What's most comforting:
A good time and good wine.
Happy, sad, love, joy
A good wine one can enjoy.
A good time and good wine.
A good wine one can enjoy.

Comforting
What's most comforting:
A piece of art.
A painting one can create.
All the longing can subside
When a piece of art can provide.

知道

她知道愛　同樣知道會失去愛
問天下癡心人有幾個
相識相愛相懷疑
離離合合從不怨
只想處得自然。

他知道愛　同樣知道會失去愛
問天下癡心人有幾個
相知相處相拖欠
緣分緣分緣分啊
永遠的懷念。

同是受傷的人
在痛苦的道上同行
也許不要了解太深
不要悲傷不要悲傷
不要流淚不要流淚。

Knowing Is Everything 1

She knew love
She knew lost love.
How many people know that?
Knowing about:
Loving, Falling apart,
No blaming, No regretting
Hoping to get along again.

He knew love
He knew lost love
Knowing, loving, suspecting.
Getting together, Hoping to last.
Predestination.

They both have been hurt,
walking on the path of pain
Maybe not understanding too much,
suffering, suffering,
crying, crying.

請妳告訴我（聽海）

你告訴我
夜夜妳心情如何
不要怕不說
憂鬱和寂寞
漂泊的妳停在那兒唷。

聽風的聲音
嘆息誰又傷了心
卻還不清醒
一定不是我
至少我冷靜。

聽風的聲音
嘆息誰又傷了心
卻還不清醒
一定不是我
至少我冷靜

聽雨的聲音

滴滴太多情
滴滴到天明
寫封信給他
當最後約定

離開的時候
想要夢什麼
夢中的一切
是怎樣的心情

Please Tell Me 1

How do you feel every night?
Don't be afraid to tell me.
Are you sad? Are you lonely?
When are you going to stop by next time?

Listen to the rain
sighing who was hurt
but not awake.
It is not me.
I am awake.

Listen to the Wind
Sighing and hurting

But not awake.
It is not me.
I am awake.

Listen to the rain.
It drizzled and drizzled
Drizzled until morning.
Write her a letter of your last decision.

Please Tell Me 4
When you leave
or want to stay and dream.
What kind of feeling is it?

Please Tell Me 7

The time to leave
Who wants him to leave,
What does she want from him?
Everything is like a dream.
What kind of feeling is it?
What is it like?

愛她（誰來愛她）

他愛她嗎　還是不愛
他們就這樣下去嗎？
見面之後還說不說話？

誰說妳愛他
見就人誇誇
妳永遠在前
從來不看他。

誰說妳愛他
妳從不提他
他在妳後面
妳從來不看他。

直到喜帖來
才知道妳愛他
不然要結婚
到底是為啥？

Loving Her

Loving Her
Does he love her or does he not
Did they speak when they met?
Did they go out for a snack?

Did they meet again?
Did they meet again?

He bragged so.
You always walked ahead.
Never paid him attention.

Who said you loved him?
You never mentioned him.
He always walks behind you.
You never paid him any attention.

Until your wedding invitation,
Then I know you love him.
You are going to get married.
What a happy surprise!

You are going to get married.
What a happy surprise!

海邊的浪

沖打白色的沙
為什麼
她臉上淚光
等不到他去擦。

他們就這樣嗎？
就讓她去吧
還是不夠堅強
勇敢去想辦法……

Only You 2

The Waves of the Ocean
The waves crashed onto the land.
Why were shining tears on her cheeks?
Why does the oil on her face stay?
Others, we can wait.

Are they going to be like this?
Let them be.
If not right
Get another opinion

情書。情書

甜蜜蜜。甜蜜蜜
情書好像巧克力
南絲不能吃
她有糖尿病
給貝蒂去吃
她不但會吃，而且做得比你的
更好吃
更好吃。

Love Poems

Love poems, love poems
Sweet as a piece of chocolate cake.
Nancy can't eat it
Because she has Type II diabetics
Better give it to Betty
She not only can eat it but also bake it.
Love poems, love poems.

就讓她去吧

海邊一定有浪
緣分比海更深更廣大
更深更廣大。

海邊的浪
沖打白色的沙
為什麼
她臉上淚光
等不到他去擦？

Let Her Be 1

There would be waves.
Predestination is more significant than the sea,
deeper and more extensive than the sea.

The Waves on the Beach
The white waves crash onto the shore
Why are there tears on her face?
Why she is not wiping the tears from her face ？

打電話

打電話
打電話
一早起來打電話
人家還沒有起床
怎能怪他不接電話。

打電話
打電話
一早起來打電話
人家還沒有起床
怎能怪他不接電話。

Telephone Calls

He never returns your phone calls.
There is an eight-hour time difference.
Just because you worry.
He was only your son and not your husband!
Time difference. Time difference.
He has his job and needs his sleep.
And he is not your husband!

熱紅紅的太陽 (熱烘烘的太陽)

熱紅紅的太陽
網上爬呀
網上爬
全家大小都看見呀

老人家呀　看連續劇呀
孫子孫女　玩遊戲呀
兒子女兒　網上工作
電腦看太久
脖子酸呀

熱烘烘的太陽
網上爬呀　網上爬
天下大事
一目了然呀
環保運動　最熱門呀
一家三代都熱衷呀。

The Red Hot Sun 1

The red hot sun shines on the Internet. Internet.
Hot Internet personalities shine so brightly.
The whole family enjoys them.

The Red Hot Sun 2
Old folks are for soap operas
The kids like games nonstop playing.
The breadwinners work so hard on the computers.
They develop computer necks and shoulders.

The Red Hot Sun
Old folks are for soap operas
The kids like games nonstop playing.
The breadwinners work so hard on the computers.
They develop computer necks and shoulders.

牽牛花

牽牛花　滿地爬
孩子們　要離家
出門辛苦要小心
前途光明笑哈哈
哈哈。哈哈。哇哈哈。

牽牛花　滿籬笆
老人年長宜在家
輕鬆，愉快，好安詳
沒有眼淚笑哈哈
哈哈。哈哈。哇哈哈。

Morning Glory

Morning glory filled the ground.
Young people want to leave home
as soon as possible.
Waha waha wahaha.

Morning glory climbed the wall.
Old folks stay home year-a-round
Easy going, plenty of fun.
No tears to shed wa ha ha
Wa ha wa ha wahaha.

Morning glory climbed the wall.
Old folks stay home year-a-round
Easy going, plenty of fun.
No tears to shed wa ha ha
Wa ha wa ha wahaha.

金山春

高高的白浪
藍藍的天空
七個小山太平洋
海鷗到處飛翔
霧中匆忙來往
一片無限春風
裝扮著太平洋

莫看那金山大橋
莫看那奧克蘭城
舊金山風華迷人
處處都有華人。
莫看那金山大橋
莫看那奧克蘭城

舊金山風華迷人
處處都有華人。

The Spring of San Francisco

The waves were high.
The sky was blue.
Seven hills of San Francisco.
The Pacific Ocean.
The seagulls were flying in the fog.
Endless spring breeze decorates the Pacific Ocean

Do not look at the Golden Gate Bridge.
Do not look at Oakland city.
San Francisco is more alluring,
Everywhere you can see Chinese.

他們散步在金山海邊

看夕陽漸漸落下寧靜水邊
雖然不久就要各起航
如此良辰美景
好友自去
意難忘，難忘……

看夕陽漸漸落下寧靜水邊
雖然不久就要各起航
如此良辰美景
好友自去
意難忘，難忘……

San Franciscian Seashore

They took a walk on the beach of San Francisco.
Watching the sunset quietly falling into the ocean.
Soon, they would go their own way.
Such a beautiful occasion.
Good friends. Old friends.
Unforgettable forever and ever.

Soon, they would go their own way.
Such a beautiful occasion.
Good friends. Old friends.
Unforgettable forever and ever.

夜留下一片安靜

海邊仍只有海鷗散步
星星在閃
海風微微
一切那樣悠悠閒閒

海邊仍只有海鷗散步
星星在閃
海風微微
一切那樣悠悠閒閒

Night Left Us the Quietness 1

Only sea gulls were on the beach.
Stars twinkled.
The sea breeze was gentle
Everything was like in a slow movie.

Only sea gulls were on the beach.
Stars twinkled.
The sea breeze was gentle
Everything was like in a slow movie.

重逢

人生何處不相逢
相逢好像在夢中
說要見面就能見面
何等緣分樂無窮

當年錦繡旗袍
慶祝過舊年
如今照片上風姿依然在

Getting Together 1

How difficult it was to get together.
They felt as if they were in a dream.
It was not easy to get together.
They came thousands of miles away.

The old satin Qipaos.
They wore them for Chinese New Year
Now, in their old pictures
beautiful as ever.

明月萬里

夜色茫茫照四周
天邊新月如勾
回憶往事
重重夢中何處求

隔千里少電信
請明月代傳訊
寄片字慰離情。

Blue Moon

The night was young and the sky hazy.
A new moon was in the sky.
Old memories alive
with the new dream.

He was thousands of miles away.
Let the moon be a messenger.
to carry a message to him.

夜模糊月朦朧

海鷗棲息海灘夢
霧氣小庭院升起
玉蘭花香大瓶裏
電視機上正演出
大型 3D 歌舞劇
隨著晚風處處送

金山夜
喜樂多
全家相聚燒烤餐
香味四溢小樓中

金山夜
喜樂多
全家相聚燒烤餐
香味四溢小樓中

The Night of San Francisco 1

The night was young.
The sea gulls rested, and the beach was empty.
The moon was hazy.
The night bloom was in the vase.
The big TV was showing
the big 3D soap opera.
The night in San Francisco was full of joy.
The whole family was having a barbecue.

The smells filled the house.
That was the night for the barbecue.
The whole family gathered for the barbecue.

The smells filled the balcony.
That was the night for the barbecue.
The whole family gathered for the barbecue.

春風吹

春風吹
春燕歸
桃杏多
遠山多青翠
湖上山花間
鳥兒雙棲又雙飛。

春風吹
春燕歸
桃杏多
遠山多青翠
湖上山花間
鳥兒雙棲又雙飛。

The Spring Wind

The spring wind is blowing
The spring swallow is returning.
Peach and pear blossoms are plentiful.
The hills are green.

The birds are singing and flying in pairs.
In pairs. In pairs.
The birds are singing and flying in pairs.

在妳左右

讓陽光
把霧霾送走
藍天下
山明又水秀
把悲哀送走
把一切煩惱丟腦後
我在妳左右。

讓陽光
把霧霾送走
藍天下
山明又水秀
把悲哀送走
把一切煩惱丟腦後
我在妳左右。

I Am Behind You

Let sunshine chase away the fog.
Under the blue sky

the mountain is green, and the water is clear.

You don't need the fog.
You don't need the rain.
Look at the blue sky.
And you have me.

You don't need the fog.
You don't need the rain.
Look at the blue sky.
And you have me.

Send the sadness away
Send it to the entrance of the lane
Don't allow it to return.

Send all the sadness away
to the main street,
all the way to town
Then let it leave on the highway
all the way to the sea.

Leave all the sadness
Leave all the sadness
Let them go
All the way to the sea.
You have me to back you up.
Don't forget that.
Don't forget that.

眼淚

為什麼她流眼淚
難道你不明白那是為了愛
要不是那有情人跟她分開
她眼淚不會流下來，流下來。

她的愛，深如海
她流眼淚是為了愛
難道你還不明白
如果不是為了愛
她的眼淚不會掉下來
掉下來。

Tears

Why did she cry?
Don't you know why?
She cried that her lover was going away.
Therefore, her tears fell and fell.

Her love, deep as the sea.
She cries for love.
Don't you understand
If it was not for love,
her tears would not have fallen.

Don't you understand
If it was not for love,
her tears would not have fallen.

Don't you understand
If it was not for love,
her tears would not have fallen.

為你唱

她要為你歌唱
唱出她心中的悲傷
因為你
你要去遠方
她要為你歌唱。

她要為你歌唱
只要有一線希望
你會回到她的身旁
她會為你歌唱。

她要為你歌唱
只要有一線希望
你會回到她的身旁
她會為你歌唱。

Sing For You

She wants to sing for you
Sing about her sadness
Because you would leave
for a faraway place.
She wants to sing for you
About her feelings.
feelings that she dared not to show.

Things did not run smoothly.
Hardships fell like falling rain.

Things did not run smoothly.
Hardships fell like falling rain.
She will sing for you
If there is a little hope that you will return to her.
She will sing for you.
No matter whether it's winter or spring summer or fall.

She will sing for you.
No matter whether it's winter or spring summer or fall.
She will sing for you.
No matter whether it's winter or spring summer or fall.

小口琴

他留下一個小口琴
就匆匆離開她
她對那小口琴情意多
朝夕相處不跟它分離。

春去秋來他沒出現
花開花落也沒出現
小口琴呀小口琴
你要怎麼安慰她？
小口琴呀小口琴
你要怎樣安慰她？

Little Harmonica 1

He left her a little harmonica
Then he left in a hurry.
She liked the little harmonica a lot
She liked it a lot.
She kept it by her side all the time.
Wishing to give it back to him when he returns.

She kept it by her side all the time.
Wishing to give it back to him when he returns.

He didn't show up spring or autumn.
He didn't appear when flowers bloom and fall.

Little harmonica, little harmonica.
What is this all about?

Little harmonica, little harmonica.
What is this all about?

他要她忘了他

他要她忘了他
要她不怨，不恨他。
不要問他為什麼。

無奈何呀無奈何
他要她忘了他
千思萬想是為什麼。

無奈何呀無奈何
他要她忘了他
千思萬想是為什麼。

He Wants Her to Forget Him

He wants her to forget him.
No complaints. No hating.
Don't ask him.
There is a reason.
He wants her to forget him.
A thousand thoughts of her

Why oh why?
A thousand thoughts of her.
Why oh why?
A thousand thoughts of her.

為什麼？為什麼？

他對她說，
"妳不能再愛我。"
為什麼？為什麼？

為什麼？為什麼？
請妳告訴我。

他對她說，
"妳不能再愛我。"
為什麼？為什麼？

為什麼？為什麼？
請妳告訴我。

Why, Oh Why?

He told her
   "You can't love me from now on."

Why? Why?
Please tell me so.

Why? Why?
Please tell me so.

小雨濛濛（一簾幽夢）

她有一樁心事
不知與誰能共
多少秘密在其中
欲訴無人能懂。

今夜小雨濛濛
秋來秋去無蹤
多少秘密在其中
欲訴無人能懂。

今夜小雨濛濛
秋來秋去無蹤
多少秘密在其中
欲訴無人能懂。

Drizzle

She has a secret
She can't share with other people.
Too many secrets.
No one can understand.

Tonight, a light rain falls
Autumn has come and left
Too many secrets.
No one can comprehend.

Tonight a light rain falls
Autumn has come and left
Too many secrets.
No one can comprehend.

Tonight a light rain falls
Autumn has come and left
Too many secrets.
No one can comprehend.

梨花淚（梨花淚）

她愛上他
永遠不後悔
除了他知心又有誰
細雨就像梨花淚
點點滴滴都嬌美

想見時滿懷甜滋味
分手時美夢難回
細雨就像梨花淚
點點滴滴都幽美。

Pear Flower Rain

She loves him, and never regrets it.
Aside from him, who really understands her.
Little rain is like pear flowers falling
Every pedal is beautiful.

When together, there is sweetness.
When parting, it's like the falling rain.
Falling rain of fallen flower petals
Every petal, a sweet memory.

When together, there is sweetness.
When parting, it's like the falling rain.
Falling rain of fallen flower petals
Every petal, a sweet memory.

太陽

吹過一颯風
帶來一陣陣寒雨
雨中小院一片翠綠
只怕春來又春去。
她有她的小路
他有他的小徑
寒雨過去
太陽會照遍大地。

她有她的小路
他有他的小徑
寒雨過去
太陽會照遍大地。

The Sun

There was a sudden wind that
brought a cold rain.
There was new green grass
suddenly appearing in the little courtyard.
She was afraid of spring coming and going too soon.

She has her directions.
He has his.
The cold rain will be gone.
The sun will come out.

She has her directions.
He has his.
The cold rain will be gone.
The sun will come out.

鵝媽媽李–春之歌

秋天將要過去
春天就要到來
春天就要到來

花兒就要開
草兒就要綠
草兒就要綠
妳要振作起來
振作起來，振作起來，妳最愛的人
現在已經在天堂
現在已經在天堂
妳現在要努力
努力陽光起來
努力陽光起來

上天的恩惠，有如無盡的大海
無盡的大海。
上天的恩惠，有如無盡的晴空
無盡的晴空。

妳們有一天
有一天終會再見面
會再見面會再見面

妳現在　要勇往直前，
努力陽光起來，陽光起來

一切都在妳眼前
在妳眼前　妳眼前　妳眼前
妳現在要勇往直前
努力陽光起來　努力陽光起來

Mother Goose Lee's Healing Song

Autumn will be over.
Spring will be here.
Spring will be here.

Flowers will bloom.
Grass will be green.
Grass will be green.

You will be happy again, happy, happy again.

Your loved one is in heaven, in heaven. In heaven.
Someday, you will meet again. Meet again. Meet again.

The fallen leaves will grow back again.
The new flowers will bloom again.
The sky will be blue again;
The clouds will be white again.

God's grace is everywhere, everywhere, everywhere.
Have faith. Have faith. Have faith
Get up and go.
Your health will come back.
You will be healthy again, healthy again, healthy again.
Have faith. Have faith. Have faith.
You'll be healthy again.
You'll be happy again.

God's grace is everywhere. Everywhere. Everywhere.
God's grace is everywhere. Everywhere. Everywhere!

大好春天

天上沒有　更白的雲
像她和他的感情
地上沒有更白茶花
像他開放她心田。

天上沒有　更白的雲
像她和他的感情
地上沒有更白的茶花
像他開放她心田。

一生沒有更美春天
向他跟隨那樣無怨
一生沒有那樣純潔
那樣無邪無怨。

一生沒有更美春天
向他跟隨那樣無怨
一生沒有那樣純潔
那樣無邪無怨。

世間總有下雨的天
當她離他越來越遠
他的掛念無邪無怨
白雲春天大好春天。

大好春天　大好春天
熱望燒著他的心田
藝術的火超越一切
超越一切無邪無怨
藝術的火超越一切
超越一切無邪無怨。

大好春天　大好春天
熱望燒著他的心田。（女高音）

大好春天　大好春天
熱望燒著他的心田。（女中音）

藝術的火超越一切
超越一切無邪無怨。（男高音）

藝術的火超越一切
超越一切無邪無怨。（男低音）

藝術的火超越一切
超越一切無邪無怨
大好春天　大好春天
熱望燒著他的心田
藝術的火超越一切
超越一切無邪無怨
藝術的火超越一切
超越一切無邪無怨。（合唱）

The Great Spring Is Here（Beethoven's Ninth Symphony）

The great spring Is here.
There is no whiter cloud in the sky.
There is no whiter flower than white camellia
that opens in her heart.

The great spring Is here.
There is no whiter cloud in the sky.
There is no whiter flower than white camellia

that opens in her heart.

The Great Spring Is Here 2
There is no more beautiful spring-like his devotion.
His feelings are more profound than the blue sky,
the blue sky of spring.

There is no more beautiful spring like his devotion.
His feelings are deeper than the blue sky,
the blue sky of spring.

There Is No Whiter Cloud 3
There are always rainy days
when she is further away.
There is always a blue sky like her art.
There iis always white cloud like her art.
The fire of her art is burning
burned by his devotion.
There is always blue sky.

There Is No Whiter Cloud 4
The blue sky of spring.
The fire of Art in the deep spring.
Burned by devotion in the deep spring.

Art.
Devotion.
The white cloud.
Blue sky of spring

There Is No Whiter Cloud 5
Art.
Devotion.
The white cloud.
Blue sky of spring. (Soprano)

Art.
Devotion.
The white cloud.
Blue sky of spring. (Alto)

Art.
Devotion.
The white cloud.
Blue sky of spring. (Tenor)

Art.
Devotion.
The white cloud.
Blue sky of spring. (Bass)

年輕的愛

移民島之婚
約翰是丹麥人，
年輕來美國，
十分不得意，
坐上了
要回丹麥的船，
回丹麥的船。
迎頭來了，
一條歐洲到移民船
船頭有一個
金髮藍眼的小女孩（喬安娜），
她向他微笑。
他馬上愛上了她。
兩人移民島上見到面，
約翰忘了回丹麥。
兩人紐約成眷屬。

Young Love

John was from Denmark.
He came to America when he was young.
He wasn't happy and thought of returning home.
While he was on a ship sailing out，
he must stop at Ellis Island.
He saw a beautiful blonde girl on a coming-in ship.
He fell in love with her（Joan）right away.
Their boats both stopped at Ellis Island.
John and Joan met and later married in New York.

啊，威斯康辛！

移民島上婚姻結果，
約翰跟喬安娜坐蓬車
遠去威斯康辛州
買了耕地幾百畝
加上生六個孩子。

Oh, Wisconsin!

John and Joan rode out to the West in a covered wagon.
They bought land in Wisconsin.
John and Joan had six children.
They bought land in Wisconsin.
John and Joan had six children.

發光的樹——死海的樹枝

六個孩子中，
老大瓊最愛冒險。
瓊的大女兒格萊萊絲，
嫁了一個黎巴嫩人，漢斯。
格萊絲跟漢斯回黎巴嫩去。
瓊也跟他們去。

瓊在黎巴嫩教書
一教三十年，
她去了以色利，
還去了死海。
來到死海邊，
看到一種沒花植物，
長成一大片，
一大片。
她採下一根，
裝在裝衛生棉的紙盒裏，
帶回美國來。
如今長成七尺高。
遮滿瓊陽台。

The Lumineer

John and Joan had six children and then divorced.
Years later, their eldest daughter Joanna liked adventures.
Joanna married a Lebanese, Hans..
Joan followed her and went to Lebanon with Joanna and
Hans.
Joan taught English in Lebanon for many years.
While there, she went to Israel, traveled throughout the
country, and even went to the Dead Sea.

Joan saw a plant by the Dead Sea.
It had no leaves or flowers but grew to be seven feet high.
Joan fell in love with the plant, broke a sprig, and
brought it home in a tampon box.
Now it is seven feet high and covers her
retirement home balcony.

家山

綠屋居。
塞爾瑪家在鄉下,
多地產。
姐姐小時候,
發高燒,
腦子受傷,
家中招一個女婿回來。
女婿的母親
搶了塞爾瑪家中地產,
使她死去的父母
至今不能合葬。

塞爾瑪請了通靈人來。
通靈的人找到她父母。
父母說
他們兩人天上在一起,很快樂,
不需要在人間合葬。
親家母也早已被原諒。

Broke Back Hills

Green House has many Chinese immigrants.
One of them is Thelma.
She has been there for five years and is a good friend of Joan.
Thelma's family had three hills. Her eldest sister was mentally disabled, and her family found a husband for her.
Her husband's mother not only took over her sister's estate but the estate of the whole family,
Thelma's sister died, and also her parents.
The mother-in-law prevented Thelma's parents from being buried in the same tomb.
Thelma was distraught. She asked a psychic who found Thelma's parents in Heaven. The psychic told Thelma that her parents were fine and together in heaven.
They do not mind if their ashes are not together. They have crossed the stream and are happy up there.
And they had forgiven the mother-in-law and wished her happiness.

菜園的太陽

貝蒂和貝拉
愛她們菜園，
買有機肥料。
種花種菜，
節省用水。
快快樂樂不嫌忙。

What's in the Garden?

Bette and Bella have lived in Green House for many years. They loved their garden in the city. Each of them had a small plot separated by an iron fence.
They shared their water source and grew native plants they used to have in their countries.

四月的愛

四月的菜園
冬天花草少。
四月，花草蔬菜長，
又嫩又新鮮，
貝拉坐在小凳子上，
看它們發芽，
然後天天長。
歡喜哇哈哈。
哇哈哇哈哇哈哈。

April Love

When the old folks in Green House have too much of
one plant, they share it with their fellow gardeners.
Bella liked to farm alone. She felt so dear to her plants,
who were her beloved friends.
She enjoyed the quietness and the sun and could see the
young plants struggling out of the soil, full of joy.

女人在愛中

簡是大醫生
退休來美國
綠屋居一住
忽已二十年，
她極愛唱歌
所有在國內，
沒機會聽到的
她在網上
都找到中文翻譯
然後在家
自己學
一天可唱幾小時。

Woman in Love

Jane, a retired doctor,
lived in the Green House for over twenty years.
If not for her daughter, who lives nearby,
she leads a lonely existence.

But she loved to sing.
Now, she has plenty of time.
She loved many songs in English
and found she could find Chinese translations of them.
She downloaded the Chinese,
She sang and sang.
She gave the new passion all.

She was a woman in love,
in love with singing.
She just found out that love is in her heart.
Maybe some of the songs are archaic,
but she felt the songs in her heart.
The love of life is in her heart.

She was a woman in love,
in love with music and songs
She'll get the song into her heart and held them tight.
It is a right now she defends
Over and over again.
It's a song to defend.
Wa ha waha wahaha.

歐瑪的膝蓋

每到週三週六
歐瑪就到綠屋居樓下去選
慈善機構特送來的各式新鮮蔬菜，
平日在斗室看看連續劇，
跳跳廣場舞，
因為膝蓋骨切除之後，
行動不是很方便。
她覺得體重增加，
雖然有女兒常常來帶她進出
她仍然覺得不甚理想。
後來看到樓下新來有勁的朋友一起唱歌跳舞，
她曾經在小學教過音樂，
就加入她們，不亦樂乎。

Irma La Knee

What is old age?
Nothing matters anymore.
Children are grown.
Grandchildren are growing.

On good old television,
the oldies are live
The new ones are just as exciting
Irma recently had hip surgery and had to stay put.
She watched movies on her old TV.
She sang along with the musicals.
Happiness is no pain in the knee.

阿里郎

溫溫是韓裔每次回韓國，
必帶新的韓劇帶子跟韓國跳舞的服裝回來，
然後教綠屋居的她的老人朋友們，
不管中國，韓國，其他外國人都會唱 "阿里
郎"。
綠屋居也成了韓國城。

A Li Lang

Wen Wen is now in her eighties.
She liked to sing Korean songs.
She invited her friends in the Green House to sing along
with her,
Suddenly, the little Green House she was in became the
Korean Town.

西班牙眼睛

芙拉是從巴拿馬來的華僑。
她父母從巴拿馬帶著她六姐妹移民到俄亥俄州。
她跟她的丈夫跑到佛羅里達州。
她老公比她小幾歲，
五十八歲時在家中心臟病發。
孩子們趕緊打電話給上班的她，
她叫急救沒用。
現在芙拉的孩子們已經長大，
她也已經七十幾歲，搬去老人院。
照顧老人院的朋友，替她煮飯，
帶她到各處老 人中心參加活動。
她記得巴拿馬運河剛剛造成，
她的父母親忙參加修建運河，很少在家，
她成天在岸上看船隻經過。
她的西班牙眼睛會等她。
等她心靈創傷恢復。
她的西班牙眼睛會等待。
等待她的恢復。

Fran's Spanish Eyes

Fran is of Chinese descent. S
She came from Panama with her parents to Ohio.
She and her six siblings settled there.
Then Fran went to Florida and married Jose.
Jose was a lot younger than her. One day, Jose had a
heart attack and died.

Tears were falling from Fran's Spanish eyes.
Please, Fran, please don't cry.
It was just adios and not goodbye.
Soon, her children will be grown.
Bring her love for her children and the old country back
to her as her heart can hold.

Fran's Spanish eyes.
Prettiest eyes in the whole world.
True Spanish eyes
They'll smile for her once again before she goes.
Soon, all the things she loved in the old country will return.
They will all wait for her and more.
They will all wait for her and more.

老鷹之歌

瑪莎是尼加拉瓜的中國移民後代。
她老公盧卡斯爸爸因為國內政變
將一家大小遷到俄亥俄州。
盧卡斯跟瑪莎在那裏
認識。

瑪莎爸爸開餐館。
盧卡斯跟瑪莎哥哥從小同學，
後來盧卡斯跟瑪莎結婚
瑪莎哥哥來加州開餐館，
老公盧卡斯跟來做廚子。
她們的孩子，孫子
都長的一表人才，進好公立大學，
學電腦，開公司……

El Condo Pasa

She'd be the daughter of a vice-president than a doctor's
wife.
Yes, she would
Yes, she could
She surely could.

She changed Martha's house into a palace
Like a mansion on a hill.
A person got tied to luxury.
Poor Martha, give it all to please the daughter of the vice
-president.
Fortunately, for just a little while
A little while.

But Maratha aimed to please
the princess who left her country.
She tried to make the princess fly high.
Fly high.
Chandeliers,
Luxury bathrooms.
Yes, she did.
Only for a little while.

快樂的家庭

潔西嘉當初移民美國，
因為老公保羅有高薪工作，
就在家養育子女。
退休後，搬來加州養老，跟學電腦，
他們做醫生的兒子，會計師的女兒都住得很近。
他們帶潔西嘉跟保羅去超市，百貨公司，餐館，
老人中心參加各種活動。
一個快樂的家庭

Happy Family

They will sing one song of their old home in China.
In summer, the folks are all happy.
By and by, wartimes will knock at their door.
Their old homes in China were abandoned.

Yes. Weep no more, my friends
Weep no more forever.
You can now sing a new song of freedom
For your old home in China.
Weep no more.
You can sing a new song in a new land
And still care about your old home.

鼎食之家

欣蒂夫家是鄭成功的後代，

母親家是曾國藩的後代。曾國藩是平太平天國
洪秀全的大臣。

亞歷山大父親就是逃太平天國從蘇州遷到長江
北部去的。他的母親奧莉維亞就是左宗棠的後
代。

亞歷山大是獨子，大學畢業就來美國，唸到博
士後。

母親戴西也是電腦博士。

他們父子兩代成家立業不容易，

兩個孩子書也唸得好，

現在都有自己的事業。

欣蒂、亞歷山大兩人退休後搬到女兒附近住。

他們在美國經濟都有基礎。他們是美國的新移
民。跟其他移民到美國的人一樣。

Rich and Powerful

Cindy's father was a descendant of Koxinga.
Her mother was a descendent of Zeng Guofan.
Zeng Guofan, the Qing Dynasty's Prime Minister, fought
against Hong Xiu Quan, the "White Long Hair" rebel
against the Qing Dynasty.
Cindy married Alex.
Alexander was a descendant of Zuo Zong Tang, who
fought the barbarians who invaded the Ming and Ching
Dynasties.

They came to America after graduating from college, got
their Ph. D.s, and then settled in America successfully.

Both their parents did not tell them the stories of their
ancestors.
Cindy and Alexander didn't tell their children in the
States either.

Now Cindy and Alex have both retired and have come to
live near their daughter.
They are all successes, at least financially, in the States.
They are new immigrants like all the other immigrants
from all over the world.

星光大道

老人居的老人中
羅麗的丈夫是喝酒被毒死。
蕭蕭的丈夫是癌症被醫院醫死。
莎莉的丈夫是緊張憂鬱自殺而死。
她們漸漸習慣。人總是要死的。
會員中白髮送黑髮的很慘
瑞麗的兒子是營造工司老闆，
28 歲被屋頂掉下壓死。
朵瑞的兒子是神經科大醫生 34 歲血癌去世。
貝蒂的兒子是在美國南部開餐館被強盜打死。
還好她們都有女兒，女兒們都住在老人院附
近。常常來看她們。
她們唱歌，跳舞，打麻將。
自己尋找樂趣。愛她們優秀的後代。
她們現在還活著都是超級老人。

Walk of Stars

In Green House
Lori's husband died of alcoholism.
Shirley's husband died of the mistreatment of cancer.
Sally's husband died of depression.
The friends gradually got used to it.
Rui Li's son died when his company's roof fell on him when he was twenty-eight.
Dori's son died of leukemia at age thirty-four when he was a neurosurgeon.
Betty's son was killed by a bandit at his restaurant.
The good thing is they all have loving daughters and beautiful grandchildren who visit them often at Green House.
They sing and dance and play mahjong.
They are alive
They are super elderly.

春天的顏色

七分鵝黃三分墨綠。
請看樹頭嫩牙的新黃，有的還有一點點新紅。
兩三天就變成鵝黃
再過兩三天，就變成新綠，然後翠綠。
多麼快樂春天的顏色。

The Color of Spring

It's spring. Leaves are 70% soft yellow and 30% new green
A couple of days later, everything turned green.
The old leaves are still there
Dark green.
Happy colors of spring.

春假

四月天，走在路上
真是山陰道上，應接不暇
忙了畫家的畫筆
這樣那樣調墨，
混合所有的顏料。
水分如不飽滿，畫不出那晶瑩的春色。
春色無邊，春色無窮

萬象更新
每時每分喚醒那無限春意。
太陽下，月光下。
清早，黃昏
春天啊春天！
多麼快樂春天的顏色！！

Spring Vacation

The mornings and evenings are all new,
full of the murmuring of the new season.
Even the rainbows are new.
We're not getting old.
We're getting newer.
We're the super elderly.

With our new exercise routines and
longer-distance walking,
no more just the river banks but up the hills.
Hills are full of new green.
And life constantly renews itself in our
children and grandchildren.
What happiness!
Spring, oh, spring!

那隻夢露貓 1

她（它）是多麼可愛。
白淨的臉
亮黑的其他全身。
最醉人的是她（它）右唇上的一個美人痣
迷人萬分。
她（它）是她（它）主人們的夢露貓。

她的主人們是調皮的大學同學。
大一開始戀愛
拿到博士才結婚。
兩人拼博士，不要孩子。

夢露貓是他們從公園撿到的一隻瘦小貓。
養了五六年，天天有機食物，
長得越來越嬌美。

歲月不饒人。
夢露貓的主人們，兩人退休了。
慢慢，老公，老妻去公園去的次數也少了。

老妻一次在一個畫攤上買到一幅一個老人抱著
一只白臉黑貓,有點像她老公抱她們夢露貓。

老妻將畫藏到閣樓。
趁老公午覺天天跑上個閣樓
在那幅白臉黑貓的嘴唇邊去慢慢畫一個像她們
家夢露貓美人痣。
因為老公患了一種眼病,無法治療
最後會模糊得看不到。
老婆除了傷心
更天天去閣樓畫那幅畫上貓唇邊的美痣。

兩年後,老公真的快看不見時,
美人痣也畫玩畢。
老婆送給老公的聖誕禮物,
就是那張美人痣的夢露貓。

老公淚眼模糊的眼睛淚流滿面。
他上了畫了。
他,她們的夢露貓跟他永恆地留在畫上。
他(她)們可愛的,永遠的夢露貓呀!

Marylyn Meowroe

Marylyn Meowroe is a beautiful cat,
born with a beauty mark above her lip,
with her dainty white face and shiny black fur and ever
so gentle purr.
Steve and Betty were college classmates.
They came to the States to continue their graduate work
and postponed parenthood.

Marilyn Meowroe was extra special.
Steve and Betty found her in a park.
She was small and fragile with a white face and shiny
black hair. They took her home.
Like their favorite star, Marilyn Monroe, the cat had a
birthmark above her little lip and an ever-soft purr,
so they named her Marilyn Meowroe.
With all the organic meow foods and tender loving care,
Marilyn Meowroe never aged in all these years they have
her.

Time goes fast.
Steve and Betty retired.
The time they went to the park became less.

One day, Betty found a picture of an old man holding a
cat on a stand in the park.
The black cat has a white face like Marilyn Meowroe but
no birthmark on her upper lip.

Betty hid the picture in the attic and
painstakingly painted a beauty mark on her upper lip like
Marilyn Meowroe.
It took her two years.

Steve developed an eye disease that could not be cured,
and his eyes would eventually go almost blind.
Betty gave Steve the picture as a birthday gift.
Steve's tears wet his face.
He could hardly see it, and he thought the picture was of
him and Marilyn Meowroe.

It was predestined that
Steve and Betty had Marilyn Meowroe for life.
And now they have the Steve and Marilyn Meowroe
picture.
What happiness it is.

原來都是愛 1

女兒們終於成了她的監護人
她愛們女兒們
女兒愛她
兩代生在不同的年代
對醫藥的看法不一。

It Was All Love

Kerry's daughters, Jane and Susie, finally became her
guardians.
It was legal. What happiness.
Kerry had to stay with her elder daughter
Jane after her husband's sudden death.
Kerry and Jane had the same temperament.
Jane said they had ADHD.
Kerry said whatever that was.
Kerry has to do everything right away or not do it at all.

哇哈哈之歌

每天定時休息
每天定時飲食
每天定時運動：
一天廣場舞
一天太極拳
一天瑜珈

每天：
做自己喜歡的事
走路
跟子女聯絡
跟朋友聊天
最最重要的
每天要快樂
哇哈哈快樂！

Walking on Sunshine

Rest adequately every day.
Eat properly every day.
Exercise every day ：
One day line dance.
One day yoga.
One day taiji.

Everyday ：
Do things one likes to do.
Get in touch with one's children.
Talk with friends.

The most important thing ：
Be happy.
Wahaha happy.

唱！唱！唱！

唱！唱！唱！
大聲唱！
用力唱！
唱好食物，不吃藥
唱將來不唱過去
不要急什麼會發生
唱！唱！唱！

唱！
在綠屋居大家唱
用任何語言唱
不要急唱不好
要開心唱到老
只要唱！一起唱！
唱！唱！唱！

音樂是長壽好藥
一天學一首歌
一天唱一個歌
活一百歲不嫌多！

Sing! Sing a song!

Sing!
Sing a song
Sing it loud
Sing it strong
Sing of good food, not medicine
Sing of the future, not the past
Don't worry about what will bring
Sing!
Sing along!

Sing!
In Green House, we sing!
All residents come and sing!
In all languages, we can sing
Don't worry if it's good enough.
Just sing, sing along!

Sing!
A song is longevity
Learn a song every day
Sing a song every day
One hundred years is not enough
Sing!
Sing along!

搖過外婆橋

我們有夢想
我們有力量。

綠屋居的朋友們大家來唱
來唱將來不是過去
相信天使也相信自己。

我們有夢
我們一起唱
我們一起高聲唱！
我們知道
時候到了
搖，搖，搖
搖過外婆橋。
哇哈哇哈哇哈哈
哇哈哇哈哇哈哈！

Across the Stream

We have a dream
A purpose in life
We have seen
the wonder of Green House.

We can take the future
Because we have a past
We believe in angels
as well as ourselves.

We have a dream
and can sing out loud.
We know when the time is right for us
We'll cross the stream
Waha waha wahaha
Waha waha wahaha!

70年重聚

七十年前
她們年十七
常常去游泳
常常去跳舞
常常出去吃東西。

如今她們八十七。
今天再次見到面。
你說高興不高興
高興高興真高興!

她們的女兒們
帶她們去吃東西。
她們從下午談到晚上。
妳說高興不高興
高興高興真高興!

七十年重聚真高興!
高興高興真高興
哇哈哇哈哈高興!

Long Long Ago

When Sally and Sarah were seventeen, they went swimming.
Then they would go dancing.
Then they would go eating.
Now, seventy years later,
Sally and Sarah are having a reunion.
Their daughters take them out to eat.
Sally and Sarah talked about seventy years ago.
from afternoon till late at night.
What a wonderful reunion!
What a marvelous reunion!
What a wahaha reunion!

小狗

小狗小狗小小狗
有人帶妳坐飛機
主人那樣地愛妳
每人見妳也愛妳。

主人送妳受訓練
被他家狗咬一口
下巴差點被咬掉
急救房間住三宿。

回來妳頑皮照舊
體重超過二十磅
妳才不過數月大
真是條美麗小狗。

小狗小狗小小狗
人見人愛不用說
等妳長到一歲大
看妳會做些什麼？

Puppy Love

Little dog, little dog,
You came with an escort.
You were so adorable.
Your owner loves you so.

Your owner sent you to be trained.
The trainer's dog bit you.
You almost lost your chin.
Three days in intensive care.

Now you are happily brought home.
Twenty pounds you have gained.
You are only a few months old.
What an amazing dog you are.

Little Dog, Little Dog,
You'll have so much love.
We all wait and see
What you can do
when you're one year old?

永遠星期六（從不星期天）

在一棟公寓裏
有一中年女郎。
她獨住公寓一間房。
每個星期六
不論風雪或冰霜
她跛腳的媽媽
必然來造訪。
媽媽腳是不方便
但還還能自己開車
上下車之困難　難以想像。
每個星期六
老媽必出現
捧著一大籃水果和甜食。
慢慢先下車。
女兒隨後出
兩人大聲笑
因為老媽耳聾有些聽不到。
母親不多留
隨即開車去
女兒不一會

必然自己也開車出去
手上拿著母親給她的食品。
不一會女兒開車回
拿著一杯辛巴克咖啡
永遠的星期六。永遠的星期六。
永遠的星期六。永遠的星期六！

Forever Saturday 1

A middle-aged woman lives in an apartment building.
She lives by herself.
Every Saturday in the early afternoon, her mother will
visit her
with a big basket of goodies,
The mother drives an SUV.
She has a handicapped sticker on her car window.
The mother only shows up on Saturday afternoon,
around three o'clock.
The middle-aged daughter will run out and meet her mother.
They'll hug and chat.
The sister only stays briefly,
She will leave when she delivers her food.
After she leaves,
the daughter-like sister will bring some of the goodies
and drive away.
She goes to the Starbucks on the main street and drinks
coffee with the goodies.

一天三餐（你提昇我）

早上吃得像皇帝
中餐吃得像大臣
晚上吃得像乞丐
長命百歲會是妳
長命百歲會是妳。

Three Meals a Day

Three meals a day.
Three meals a day.

Eat breakfast as a king.
Eat Lunch as a premier.

Eat dinner as a beggar.
Or just drink water.

Smile and laugh if you can.
Smile and laugh all the time.
All the time.
All the time.

天氣真晴朗

今天天氣好
老人起來早
綠屋太陽照
大家來歌唱

來歌唱
來歌唱
大家來歌唱！

麥克風裝好
手機準備好
不需要銀幕
空牆就夠了！

妳先唱
我後唱
他再唱
然後大合唱！

哇哈哈
哇哈哈

哇哈哈

哇哈哇哈哇哈哈！

Sing a Song

Today the weather is fine.
Old folks got up early.
The sun is shining.
Let us sing.

Let us sing
Let us sing
Let us sing

Let us sing all together!

Set up the microphone!
Open the cellphone
There is no need for a screen
Just an empty wall is enough.

You sing first
He sings next
I can sing in the third.

Wahaha
Wahaha
Wahaha…..
Waha waha wahaha!

天天來跳舞

讓我們來跳舞
從下午跳到黃昏，我們不會累。
我們不會累！

我們八十幾
我們有舞伴
這裏沒別人
我們有自己！

有人彈鋼琴
有人吹口琴
一齊打個轉
沒人會跌跤！

我們來學習
我們來跳舞
一直跳到晚
我們一直跳到晚！

不管人家怎麼講
我們只管做自己。

不管人家沒勇氣
我們只管做自己
人生難得幾回喜
我們只管跳自己
四步、三步、森巴、倫巴、方塊舞、廣場舞……
來！來！來！
大家一起來
一起來跳舞！

我們來跳舞
我們來跳舞！
跳完舞！吃包肥！
慶生會！天天慶生會！
天天來跳舞！
偶爾吃包肥！
天天來跳舞！天天慶生會！

Dancing

Let's keep dancing
From afternoon till evening.
Are we everlasting
Or is this the first time?

We're in our eighties.
I'll be your dancing partner.
Nobody else was in the room.
We are happy ourselves.

She's got her hands on the keys.
She's playing the harmonica
Spin around if you want.
We know we are not falling.

We can learn a little about everything.
Let's keep on dancing
Right here until evening.
We are everlasting.

Next time. The same thing.
Don't give a damn of what people are thinking.
They don't know what they are missing.
This kind of movement is rare.
They don't know what they are missing.
People poke their heads in
to see what we are doing.

The Fox-trot, the Waltz, Samba, Rumba, and Square
Dancing.
Come in and join.
You will not be regretting.

We keep on dancing!
We keep on dancing!
After that, we'll have a big dinner and celebrate.
Celebrating life,
That's what we are doing.
Celebrating life,
We are dancing.

地下室

老房子
新主人
要重修

地下室中發現了
一個大保險箱。
裡面啥東西？
沒有人知道。
老主人已經去世。

做事工人離去了
保險箱入銀行手裏
入銀行手裏。
哇哈哈，哇哈哈。
哇哈哇哈哇哈哈

Ballad of the Basement

There was an old house with a basement.
The new owner wants it renovated.
The workers found a safe box in the basement.
Waha waha wahaha.

It was sealed in the safety box.
No one knows what's in it.
It can't be opened because of the old owner is deceased.
It became the property of the bank.

What's in it no one knows.
The workers disappeared.
To this day, only the bank knows
Only the bank knows.
Waha waha wahaha…

復活節的慶祝

大家從來沒有穿得這麼美。
綠屋局在開復活節派對。
有菜有酒。有歌有舞。
教堂前白玉蘭特別白。
教堂鐘聲特別美！

春天到！復活節到！
復活節帽在那裡？
不要緊。海倫會摺紙。
她幫大家摺紙帽
只要幾張紙。

我們的復活節遊行
在我們的長走道裏
我們吃復活節包肥
"安全道" 免費送的！

我們一人有一個
兔子紙袋子

裡面都是兔子巧克力
本地糕點店免費送的！

我們復活節遊行隊來了
我們復活節遊行隊來了
我們跳舞，我們唱
等下給妳看影像！
哇哈哇哈哇哈哈！

Easter Parade

Never was everyone dressed up so pretty.
Green House is having an Easter Party.
There were songs and wine.
The church bells sounded extra crispy.
The magnolia flowers in front of the church were extra
white.

Spring is here. And Easter is here.
Where is everyone's Easter bonnet?
No matter. Helen knows paper mache.
She can turn out paper bonnets in no time.

We'll have an Easter Parade
Up and down the long hallway.

We'll have our Easter buffet
Donated by local Safeway.

Easter songs we'll sing.
We each get a small Ester bunny paper mache.
Chocolate eggs we'll have
Thanks to a local pastry shop.

Here comes our Easter Parade.
Down our long hallway.
Down our long hallway.
Wa wa wahaha!

畫家之歌

要畫什麼？
現在是春天。
百花齊放。
紅梅桃李
水仙，白合
玉蘭，梔子……

誰能背叛自然？
迎春花一開
冰雪不露面
用畫筆慶祝
十彩顏色開。

A Song on Canvas

What does she want to paint,
All the flowers are blooming.
The plum, peach, and pear.
Daffodils and peonies.

All are blooming
All are colors.
A song on canvas
It's a song of colors.

Who can disobey nature?
When the crocus came out,
the snow will melt.

Let's sing with our brush,
a brush of technicolor.

牡丹花后

牡丹太雍容華貴
要用啥法襯托？
葉子一筆不能錯。
勾筋更不用說。說時時間快
下筆麻煩多，一不小心顏色弄錯一切要重新過。

Queen Peony

Queen Peony,
Queen Peony
If you know how hard it is to draw her.

The preparation is not hard.
It's the color you can't control
on the paper.

Whether it's dry or wet.
One second passed
The painting is ruined.

Try it once
Try it twice
You will finally get the hang of it.

Then the queen will bow to you,
cause she knows you've tried it
500 times.

上午初晴

下午有風
風尚未來
花先飛起
落花片片
嫩葉加深
先黃後綠
能不歡欣
能不歡欣。

下午一到
風就刮起
花先飛起
一片畫雲
嫩葉加深
爭出風頭
好不熱鬧
春回大地。

Oh, Good Morning

Oh, Good Morning. Oh, Good Morning.
The sun rose early, not as usual.
Because it's a leap day.
Maybe that is why? Maybe that is why,
Clementine.

The flowers are blooming.
The petals are falling.
The petals are flying over the sky.
She tried to catch them
without much success.
She returned home
and painted them.
She returned home and painted them.
She painted them
Clementine.

Painting them is not as much fun
as catching the pedals.
If you haven't tried it.
It's high time
To have the fun,
Clementine.

啊！好美的早晨

穿廊有一絲微風
穿廊有一絲微風。
早晨晴朗像蜂鳥穿進穿出，
尋找它的蜜糖。

啊， 好美麗的早晨
啊，好美麗的一天
我有歡樂思想
今天我一切吉祥。

我的鄰居都在打掃。
我的鄰居都在練習。
我想趕快把我音樂書打開，
今天音樂老師一定會來。

啊，好美麗的早晨。
啊，好美麗的一天。
我們今天會學一首新歌。
那就是"我的夢想"。

我們中心主食牛肉酸白菜。

那會很好吞咽

然後星巴克咖啡。

濃濃全脂的鮮奶

啊！一切正中我口味。

啊！一切都讓我開懷。

啊！這樣美麗的一天。

這樣美麗的一天！

Oh, what a beautiful morning

There is a cool breeze over the balcony,
There is a cool breeze over the balcony,
The morning is as fresh as the humming birds busy finding their nectar.

Oh, what a beautiful morning.
Oh, what a beautiful day,
I got a beautiful feeling
The music teacher is coming over today.

All the neighbors are doing their exercises.
All the neighbors are doing their exercises.
Better get my music book ready.
Cause I think our music teacher is coming over today,

Oh, what a beautiful morning.
Oh, what a beautiful day.
We will be learning a new song today
And it's called "I Have a Dream."

We will have corn beef and cabbage today,
It will be tasty and easy to chew.
Then we'll have Starbucks coffee latte.
Everything is going my way.
Oh, everything is going my way,.

我有夢想

我有夢想，使我成長。
我的夢想，很短很簡單。
我要健康，我要繼續成長。
我要訓練我的身體，頭腦。

我要健康，我要有用
我要幫助我的朋友
我要每天微笑面對
所有困難，所有失望。

我相信命運，不會恐懼。
我會知道那天時間來臨。
我會穿越銀河世界。
我會沒有任何恐懼。

我愛我家，我愛朋友。
她，他們是我最好依靠。
有時我們思想不一，
但是我永遠愛著他們。

我愛唱歌
我愛舞蹈
我愛與朋友一起享受。

我們只需要
一間小屋。
我們唱歌
我們舞蹈
我們只需要 一間小屋。

I Have a Dream

I have a dream, a dream of my own.
It's happy, short and it's sweet
My health is good, my appetite is great.

I sleep well, and I do my exercises.
I will stay healthy and be helpful to myself
and people around me.
I'll sing whenever I please.

I believe in angels, Something good in
everything I see.

I believe in angels
When I know the time is right for me.
I'll cross the stream.
As I please.

I love my family. I love my friends.
They are dear to me, all the time.
If we don't agree all the time.
I love them just the same.
If we quarrel sometimes
We love one another just the same.

I love singing, I love dancing.
I am always happy when I sing and dance.
I love to sing with friends. That's what we do all the time.
We sing songs together and forget about pain.

A little room is all we need
Where we sing, and we dance.
A little room is all we need.
When we sing, and we dance.

新冠狀病疫四朵金花

多運動　多睡覺
多喝水　多開心
哇哈哈　開心最重要。

Three mores for COVID patients

Exercise more Sleep more
Drink more water Care More about other people
Wahaha be optimistic above all.

新冠狀病疫三少

少去人多處
少煩心
少生氣
哇哈哈老人新冠病毒不用急。

Three lesses for Covid patients

Less participation in crowds
Lees worrying
Less stress
Wahaha, seniors can ward off COVID-19.

夏天到

夏天到了，太陽曬得更多了。
身體也更健康了。
農夫市場新鮮蔬菜滿攤。
各種水果莓子甜又香。
院子裏燒烤
西瓜、玉米甜似糖。
假如妳在附近請來嚐。
隨時都歡迎。
請來一起唱唱歌
乘乘涼。

夏天到，日子長，
睡個午覺不嫌多
晚上好看大月亮。
大家一起來唱歌
快樂又清爽。

Summertime

Summer is here. There is more sunshine.
Our health is improved.
There are all kinds of fresh veggies and fruits.
The corn is sweet for barbecuing.
You can come without getting invited.
You are welcome all the time.
Come and sing a song.
Come and dance a dance.
Just drop by and have a little fun.

Summer is here and days are lengthening.
A little afternoon nap is in order.
The big moon is worth watching at night.
Sing a serenade.
Happy summer night.
Happy summer time.

老妻癡呆

他能感覺她的身體
當他，她們躺在一起。
他不能思想。
十年前醫生就將她判了死刑。

他感到憤怒。
他愛的火焰仍然燃燒。
他為什麼不將她送養老院。
他為什麼學不到？

舊愛，不能送她入院。
他知道他不現實。
她現在如同植物。
但是，舊愛。
他從前怎樣的愛。

他感到憤怒
他愛的火焰仍然繼續。
他知道她會越來越糟。

但是
他不能放棄
他的舊愛。
舊愛，不能離開他的舊愛。
回家吧，舊愛。

Old Love

He can feel her body
When they are lying in bed.
Too much confusion
Going around through his head.

And it makes him so angry
To know that the flame still burns
Why can't he give her up?
When will he ever learn?

Old love, can't leave her alone.
But he knows that it's not real.
Just an illusion.
She's not but a piece of vegetable.
But he was used to what he always felt.

And it makes him so angry
to know that she'll get worse and worse.

He'll never get over
He knows he'll never learn.

Old love, can't leave her alone.
Old love, go on home.

老人中心卡拉 OK1

三十年前闊人家的少爺

闊人家的少爺

個個怪模樣

最喜歡

夏威夷 T 衫

頭髮梳得像飛機場

一條紅手帕

插在西裝口

在人面前聳肩膀，

吹口哨，腦袋晃

哇哈哈，現在也一樣。

Senior Center Karaoke 1

The playboy thirty years ago,
Now wears Stange jackets and trousers
A Hawaiian shirt and airplane hairdo
A folded red handkerchief tucked in the jacket pocket.
Whistled and shrugged shoulders.
Wahaha, still the airplane hairdo.

老人中心卡拉 OK2

三十年前的十里洋場
坐汽車。住洋房
跳舞，唱歌，
有情男女一雙雙，
洋場十里好風光。
現在呢。時髦學的好像，
哇哈哈上海好風光。

Senior Center Karaoke 2

The city thirty years ago.
A Ford, A highrise.
Social dancing and singing..
Lovely couples, dancing and singing..
Nowadays Online dancing and singing.
Wahaha on-line dancing, singing and everything. …
wahaha….

老人中心卡拉 OK3

她是浮萍一片
漂泊在人生大海
獨自陶醉在幽靜的夜晚……
現在
獨自陶醉在幽靜的夜晚
對著電視、電腦、手機
與月兒星星對話……
三十年前的情景
三十年後……
哇哈哈獨自獨自……

Senior Center Karaoke 3

She was a piece of waterweed
and drifted on the water.
Alone, she drifted in the dim light.
She drifted, facing the moon and the stars.
Now she drifts with the TV, movies, and cell- phones.
And talks to the moon and stars.
The same scenario as in the past.
Same scenario
Wahaha, not too bad, the same scenario, Wahaha

老人中心卡拉 OK4

輕輕春風遙遙相思
輕輕春風拂面
枯萎愛情不再青蔥
如夢一般往事，今夜回夢中。舊歌好聽
好夢依舊
大家來聽，大家來唱
好不痛快，好不輕鬆……
哇哈哈
好不痛快，好不輕鬆……
哇哈哇哈哇哈哈。

Senior Center Karaoke 4

Gentle spring breeze,
Far away longings,
Lost love withers.
Old memories are gone, and
will be in her dreams.
Dreams, Sweet dreams,
Let's sing about the future and not the past.
Wahaha…
Sing about the bright future.
About the bright future, we sing.

老人中心卡拉OK5

老古董
糊塗又冬烘
教訓兒女不放鬆
女兒不許交際
兒子要上常春藤大學
老古董呀老古董……

Senior Center Karaoke 5

Old man. Old man.
Stubborn and old- fashioned.
Strict about raising his children.
The daughters should go to a Community College.
The sons go to an IVY League College.
Wahaha, the daughters go to community college.

老人中心卡拉 OK6

田園之歌
看雨後晴
天飄白雲
村姑帶斗笠
留在農村的懷抱
不受都市的煩惱
樹下乘涼把扇搖
炊煙繞樹梢……

Senior Center Karaoke 6

The rain stopped
The white cloud was in the sky.
The country maiden is wearing a straw hat
And she stays behind.
She will not be bothered by the city noise.
She leisurely cools herself with a straw fan.
She'll cook the evening meal outside.
Wahaha, she'll cook the evening meal outside.

月亮光

拉開窗，月光光亮。
像蠟燭從天空照著
牆上明鏡光
失去的日子，一年復一年。
她已無言語可形容
什麼能使她，他們快樂。
她已經試過一切。
從所有角度試過。
她檢查自己所有的懷疑
她了解她沒有站腳地方。
月亮呀，月亮……

Moon Light

She opened up the blinds again
And let the autumn moonlight in
To light the candles hanging from the sky
The mirrors on the walls reflect
The days she has lost, the years she had led
She's waking through a million miles away.
There is nothing in the world they say
That makes him and her happy anyway
She counted all the days that she had tried
She has looked through all the angles, and
She questioned all the doubts she had
She realized there was nothing here for her.

永遠不離開

朝陽裏，她不能講
許多事，她不能講。
她有多愛他。
他是否愛她？

事情那樣地遙遠，
他好像那麼近，又那麼遠。
他不在時，她想擁抱他，
她想知道　，他也想擁抱她。
她要知道，他對她是否
一樣想法？
如果如此，
她將永遠不要離開他。

他的周圍太複雜，
光芒耀眼她眼瞎。
燈光下他出現
怎能知道是真的他。
他那樣那樣遠⋯⋯

怎能知道是真的他……

真的他……

真的他……

Stay Forever

In the morning sun. She couldn't tell him.
She couldn't tell him so many things.
About how much she loved him.
About how much he really meant

It's so far away, but it's so easy to see him.
When she was away, she wanted to put her arms around
him.
And she wants to know if he feels the same.
Cause if he does, she wants to stay forever.
And she wants to know if he feels the same way.
Cause if he does, She wants to stay forever.

There are so many colors that surround him.
Some so bright that she can hardly see.
A light reflects on all the things that make him real.
Things that make him truly free.

So far away. So far away.

多加一點點

一等一兩年
不是不愛憐
只是再需要
那麼一點點。嘴巴甜一點，
就是個木瓜，只曉得賺錢。
只是再需要
那麼一點點。嘴巴甜一點
就是個木瓜，只曉得賺錢。

Just a Little Bit More

She waited for him
One year after the other.
Not that he wasn't loving.
Not that he wasn't caring.
She had wanted just a little bit more.
Wahaha, just a little bit more.
A few sweet words,
A single rose,
A kiss behind the ears.
Just a little more.
Wa ha wa ha wahaha.

小秋香

暖和的太陽照過小秋香
春姐爸爸愛
夏姐媽媽愛
只有小秋香
整天工作忙
掃地搭桌
勤快，可愛
可愛的小秋香……

Rachel

The warm sun was shining on little Rachel.
Dad loves Daisy.
Mom loves Summer.
Only Rachel works all day.
She sweeps the floor and cleans the table.
diligent and happy.
Rachel, Oh Rachel, diligent and happy.
Wahaha, hard-working and happy Rachel.

鄰居的狗

天色已暗
他還在院子裏
逗狗玩
狗大概要睡了，
不肯接球。
球滾到街上去了。
他追上去，
看街上的車子，
有沒有她的灰色 SUV。
出差幾天，
她說昨天就回來的……

What's the Dog in the Neighbor's Yard

The sun was setting.
The dog was still in the yard.
It was tired, maybe wanting to sleep.
It didn't want to catch the ball.
The ball ran to the street.
He went to get the ball rolled under a parked car.
He was looking for his wife's gray SUV.
She was supposed to be back yesterday.
Wahaha, the little dog does not want to play.
It wanted his mistress to be home and then play.

夕陽

老太太來西部
夕陽西下好散步,
人行道上來回,來回走
等到媳婦做好飯,
兒子來叫她。
老太太,走路胃口好。
多吃一點不會胖。
哇哈哈再走 200 步。

住煩了回東部
好像足球進了網。
出去散步有耐心
多走幾步不會胖。
像打游擊不知勝負。
在外消磨不驚慌。一下夕陽已西下。
她已穿了厚夾克
一切免驚慌。
女兒一點不著急。
讓老媽在外面張望。夕陽西下,下去了。

一家先上桌吃飯。

讓老媽回來自己熱湯，熱飯。

再等幾秒太陽西下……

太陽已經下山崗……

Sunset

The old lady walking when the sun was going down.
She knew the sun was going down.
She entertained herself until the sun was going down,
waiting for her daughter-in-law to cook dinner.
She knew her son would call her
then she could go home and eat.

Two hundred more steps.
Man, She knew how the sun was going down.
Man, she knew how it went down.
Might get a little impatient; just wait until the sun went
down.

Underground, any city she visits with her children. is a
touchdown.
Getting to the dough like a sweet, sticky ball.
The East Coast is not like the West Coast.
Two o'clock is late.
She has a, heavy jacket and doesn't feel worried.

But, her daughter will take it easy.
She'll just let her old mom stay out until it is dark.
The whole family will eat without her.
And Mom can reheat the soup and the rice
Wait a little, wait, the sun goes down. The sun is going
down....

關於《新大陸叢書》

　　長期以來，所謂的"海外華文文學"，除了香港這個特殊環境的地區外，所指的不外是台灣和大陸的延伸而已。對於外國人及土生土長或長期居住在海外的華人以中文創作的作品，常被有意無意地忽略了，當然這是我們的看法！

　　無疑，目前"海外華文文學"的大部份作品是由台灣、大陸在海外的作家所組成，其實土生土長和其他地區的華人作品應該更能反映海外華人文學的精神面貌。他們的水準容或參差不齊，但優秀作品必然有其留傳的價值。況且隨著中文地位在世界上的提高，這種歷史現象應該得到肯定。

　　基於此，本刊決定出版《新大陸叢書》，提供詩友自費出版的管道，並以長期居住於海外的華人作品為主，從新詩作為整個計劃的開始，將"海外華文文學"有系統地加以整理、推廣。

　　　　　　　　　　　　——新大陸詩刊

*郵購以上書籍，每冊國內請加空郵郵費$4.00，國外$7.50。寄：
329 La Paloma Ave., Alhambra, CA 91801, U. S. A

鵝媽媽李歌舞集

新大陸叢書之五十六

作　　者：王克難

封面畫作：王黎輝 Sofia Yu

發 行 者：新大陸詩刊

329 La Paloma Ave.
Alhambra, CA 91801
U. S. A.

初　　版：2024 年 8 月

Mother Goose Lee's Song and Dance Anthology
1st edition
Claire Wang – Lee

Printed in the USA
CPSIA information can be obtained
at www.ICGtesting.com
CBHW060330231024
16239CB00054B/742

9 798331 084158